Board Governance:
Social Profit Biz Basics

*Everything I Needed In Business I
Learned in the Bathroom*

Board Governance: Social Profit Biz Basics

Everything I Needed In Business I Learned in the Bathroom

Thyonne Gordon, Ph.D

First Printing: 2015

ISBN 978-1-889210-10-0 PAPERBACK
ISBN 978-1-889210-11-7 ELECTRONIC

A Writer Space Publishing
4859 W. Slauson Ave. #299
Los Angeles, CA 90056

www.awriterspace.com
www.beyondstory.com

Honoring The
Leaders

Taking the stand to lead the way to the future.

This is in recognition of board chairpersons whom I have served under and their commitment to organizational excellence
Brett Bouttier, CoachArt
Zander Karmin, CoachArt
Kenneth Karmin, A Place Called Home
Bob Israel, A Place Called Home
Peter Gilhuly, Esq., A Place Called Home

* * * * *

And Dedicated To
My Lovely Daughter
Matthia B. Sales
A leader from the beginning

Contents

Introduction

For each book in the Business Basics for Social Profit Sector from Infrastructure to Money and Marketing – there has been a consistent theme in which successful social profits operate. That theme is that the people behind the organization are what make the organization successful. Board Governance is no exception. Follow these easy to read bathroom to business tips and invigorate your board of directors and the work that they do.

As a graduate of three highly esteemed institutions, I learned a lot at each. However, it was the lesson I learned through the guidance of a mentor to "start in the bathrooms" that was surprising to me. This lesson would become a constant tool in how I managed business efforts in the future.

Board Governance: Social Profit Biz Basics

Imagine the surprise of the staff that my first and most important meeting began with my cleaning and maintenance crew. And, imagine the shock of my realization that learning about this business would come from such a discreet and unsuspecting place. Well flush me away (pun intended)!

Using the simple lessons in Everything I Needed To Know in Business I Learned in the Bathroom: Board Governance will enliven your board as they understand their roles and opportunities as board members. It will also help grow your board of directors into the successful team that supports you.

The book in its standard format – divided into three parts. An easy to read guide that quite frankly, can be finished behind a closed door on a familiar seat – in the bathroom!

501c3
The Business of Heart, Head & Soul

In this world where business is measured by a Wall Street status or how much companies make and take, I believe a shift must occur. This shift is based on the heart of a business. I know, many might note business, as an entity, does not have a heart. I believe business is a creative energy of people giving it heart.

With every client that's served, dollar that's earned and vendor that's affiliated, a steady beat occurs that gives the business a conscious how and why existence. And the beats are measured such that when there is a misstep, it causes a skip in that beat – and accordingly damage to that heart and ultimately to the business overall.

Starbuck's became one of fastest growing companies in the '90s be- cause of the pulse Howard Schultz shepherded. When he left and the company's beat began to go off, it was evident that the heart of the company was no longer the same. Upon his return he began to monitor and secure the steady socially conscious heartbeat of the company returned too.

That heartbeat is in every company and becomes evident as culture. Starbuck's culture happened to be a distinct care of the product and the customer as important. It was the type of beat that caused employees to care about not just the company, but the customers the company served. In his book, "Onward: How Starbucks fought for Its Life Without Losing Its Soul," Schultz shares the story of an employee who gives a kidney to a regular customer. Yes, that sounds above and beyond the call of duty for any employee, but it wasn't just because that employee was a good person (and yes, they were great) but it was because of the culture that Starbucks created around care – care for each cup of coffee and care for each customer.

When we begin to focus on what value there is in giving goods and services as well as what we receive in return, we can grasp what a company's heart beat feels like.

The idea is not so far fetched. The giving begins with offering quality products and services for reasonable and fair pricing. However, it extends to being in sync with the communities in which our businesses reside as well as understanding and valuing the needs of the consumers.

There is enough to go around--if we are not so greedy as to hoard the extras.

In this equation of socially conscious businesses, the industry that society has labeled as "not for profit or nonprofit" organizations, have the opportunity to lead the way. These organizations understand the cause and affect of giving and the strong and steady heartbeat began at the inception of the idea to formulate a 501c3. These are the organizations that prioritize giving as a means of operating. Yet, as much as the giving aspect is understood, receiving and considering the core of such a business is often misinterpreted. A key element is evident in the label that begins with lack. And that lack projects a weakened heartbeat leading towards a needy trajectory verses a confident life changing one.

The 501c3 space is the only industry that is described by what is "not" done verses what "is" done. In this inaccurate affront to an industry providing on-purpose services and products, the public tends to view such organizations as poor and needy (just as much in need as the constituents served).

With this impoverished mentality it is no wonder the difficulty 501c3's have acquiring funds for excellent services provided for society to work more holistically.

In general 501c3's are viewed as beggars. Yet, in truth, every business "asks" for something and the true test in consumerism is whether or not the company delivers when the "ask" is met.

In my work in this space, I encourage organizations providing on-purpose services to stand up for their work with a strong heartbeat, which starts with embracing titles that better inform the work. Changing the labels that others have put on 501c3's is the first start to not only building stronger infrastructure, but also in empowering the entire community affiliate – employees, constituents and donors.

In the Everything I Needed In Business I Learned in the Bathroom book series, these organizations have been relabeled as Social Profit Organizations. This is my own personal way of correcting the skip in the beat of the heart in the service community. This is the beginning of the shift I encourage.

Join me in uplifting the powerful work of Social Profit Organizations as positive and inspiring, by choosing our words carefully and specifically focused towards making a difference.

Enjoy the series and I look forward to hearing your feedback.

Chapter One:
Secure Your Board Duties

Bathroom: Must be in located in a secure and reliable place

Business: The board is the secured and steady holding tank of the organization

Serving on a nonprofit board can be a rewarding experience. Those who have served report that they not only feel a sense of responsibility but there is also something euphoric about being a part of something that is working towards the greater good. The work of board members can be extensive and tedious however, most find that even though there's a lot of work to be done, it's for a good cause.

Board members are responsible for the fiduciary well-being of the organization and that responsibility begins with understanding and fulfilling the mission. The mission of any good social profit is the core service that the organization provides for the common good. It is from the mission that the culture, programs and teams of people develop into what I call a purpose driven social profit.

On some occasions, a founder of a social profit brings a board together at its beginnings and asks for assistance in creating the mission statement. These organizations tend to have very active and committed boards of directors because they have actually participated in the creation of the organization from its start.

However your board of directors came into play, they all have come together to assure the organization remains in existence for years to come. As your board joins together to support your organization, there are some key duties that they are emboldened to. Though there are many activities that boards can participate in there are three primary duties of any social profit board. These functions are constant and should always be taken care of. Just like a bathroom needs to be in a secure and steady place like a house or office building, your social profit board needs to be a steady force in the organization. To achieve and assure this, the board is guided by three duties.

1. *Duty of Care: A board member must exercise reasonable care when making decisions for the organization.*

    It is the responsibility of each board member to participate in decision-making on behalf of the organization. Board members are to act individually in this decision-making and make independent judgments while doing so. Decisions must be informed which means as a board member you have done your due diligence in being familiar with all relevant and available facts of the issue.

Management of the organization play an important part in this Duty of Care as board members rely on the organization's management to provide timely and sufficient information such that board members can make informed decisions. As a board member, if you find the information being provided is insufficient or incomplete, it is your job to "take care" and question information before making final decisions.

This may seem insignificant in every day matters such as what time you may open or close a facility, but practicing the Duty of Care in small things prepares you for the challenges that may come in the future. How would you respond as a board member to the buying or selling of a significant asset? What if you were entering into a substantial material contract that could cost the organization it's 501c3 status?

Having a firm policy around Duty of Care begins with paying attention to the little things; following a decision making protocol (i.e. Roberts Rules of Order); and being in compliance with good practices around standard Duty of Care. In corporate compliance, Duty of Care requires that board members "attempt in good faith" to assure that:

a. A corporate information and reporting system exists;

b. Reporting system adequately assures that appropriate information for compliance with applicable laws, will come to the attention of the board in a timely manner;

c. Compliance with any and all laws and statutes in field (i.e. social services requires reporting of suspected abuses with child care facilities)

Having a protocol and clear understanding of Duty of Care for board members, can assure information is properly disseminated and reviewed thus supporting the organization in the most effective and caring manner available.

2. *Duty of Loyalty: This duty requires a board to affirmatively protect the interests of the organization and imposes an obligation to refrain from conduct, which would injure the organization.*

Within the Duty of Loyalty, a board member must never use information gained from their board position for personal gain. Instead, they must always act for the best interest of the organization.

Board members set aside their own interests when making decisions on a board for an organization. The personal, professional and other interests – perhaps from other affiliations – are set aside for the good of the board that one is serving. Simply put, the social profit organization comes first and board members should refrain from opportunities for personal gain.

A breach of Loyalty also exists if a board member fails to preserve the confidentiality of an organization's business. Confidentiality is of utmost importance because disclosing information to outside individuals may jeopardize opportunities for the organization. Directors must avoid any conflict between duty and self-interest. Divided allegiances are the major cause of loyalty breach.

3. *Duty of Obedience: A board member must be faithful to the organization's mission statement. The must act in a way that's consistent with the organization's goals.*

Compliance with the obligations inherent in the duties of obedience can protect a social profit board of directors from legal implications. Decisions of the board are to be independent, informed, non-biased and in good faith to the best interest of the corporation. As long as these standards are met, the board cannot be challenged in court.

This is presumed and called "the business judgment rule" and is the standard application unless there is evidence showing a board member has a conflict of interests that was not disclosed or a vested interest in a transaction. A basis for this rule is the trust that the public holds that the organization will manage donated funds properly.

As board members are committed to the organization's mission, they maintain their duty of obedience and thus make their social profit organization a strong viable service oriented part of the community.

The basic duties of the board should be reviewed with every board member. And, you have probably heard that your board members have a fiduciary responsibility to the organization. Though commonly quoted, many times it is not understood what this means. Just how does this fiduciary responsibility fit in with the duties of a board member?

Fiduciary Responsibility of Board Members

When entering into a relationship of trust or confidence, you become a fiduciary to the organization or persons that you are entering the relationship with. A fiduciary relationship with an organization is one-sided. That means that the relationship is designed to meet the needs of the organization and not the person supporting the organization. As outlined in the duties of a board member, the fiduciary must act without regard to his or her own needs.

Board members are entrusted with overseeing the fulfillment of an organization's mission and must be principally concerned about the organization and how it performs.

Thyonne Gordon, Ph.D

In short, to have a fiduciary responsibility means the board has a legal and ethical responsibility. They put the organization above their own needs for the good of the organization. This requires board members to be objective and unselfish in decision making. According to Board Source it requires, *"Honest, trustworthy and efficient board members acting as stewards of public trust, always acting for the good of the organization."*

Understanding Breeds Success

As you understand these duties better, you might also understand why your board members joined forces to assist your organization. Note that people who join boards normally do it with a worthy goal in mind. Knowing the great weight of responsibility that your board has might prompt you to thank them more often. It should also prompt you to make sure your board is well aware of what they've signed on for. Review the duties of a board with your board members at least annually.

When board members are equipped with understanding of what they have been recruited to do, they can act more responsibly to their call of duty. Educate your board with this information and more. Finally, you're your board to survey themselves so that they know what they've signed up for. Many times board members think being on the board is just about checking on the management. It's important that they also know it's about checking in with themselves too.

As a learning tip from the bathroom, I'd say make sure your organization's foundation is built with strong, steady and trustworthy individuals – just like your bathroom is built. In the bathroom, cement secures the fixtures that you don't want to move. The Duties of the Board are your security for success.

Chapter Two:
The People Who Make It Happen

Bathroom: Many parts make the bathroom function as a bathroom.

Business: Many people are required to help an organization function effectively.

The most critical part of a functioning building or place is the parts that hold it together. This is especially true for the bathroom. It's amazing how many intricate parts the bathroom has to make it what it is. Just the basics of a toilet, sink and shower let you know there is a functioning room to serve various purposes. But if you broke each of these elements down, there are even more parts.

Take for example the toilet. It has a tank, trip lever, toilet bowl, toilet seat and all the parts in the tank and that hold the toilet down on the floor. Bolts, handles, and levers – the toilet requires many parts to make it work. This example relates directly to your social profit.

Your business requires so many working parts and so many working people, to make sure it's functioning properly. The people that serve on your board of directors are just a subset of how the organization operates but an important subset.

The board of directors literally is part of the foundation of your business. Your social profit paperwork could not be filed without knowing at least three of the members of your board – Chairperson, Treasurer and Secretary. That is how important the board is to the organization. The government doesn't even grant you 501c3 status without knowing there is a board holding the accountability.

It is the board of directors who hold the fiduciary responsibility and they are committed to assuring the organization not only fulfills its' mission but also stays fluent and afloat.

The board of directors holds themselves, and the organization accountable for the work of the cause. Having a strong and informed board of directors is the crux to having effective programs, people, marketing, infrastructure and money.

But how do you find people who are committed, responsible, honest and ready to support your organization? Board recruitment is a major part of running a social profit organization and should no be considered lightly.

Board Recruitment

Many organizations struggle with getting highly qualified and enthusiastic people to commit to board service. Yet, what's more important to sustain your organization than having great board members? Board recruitment is probably one of the most important priorities every organization has. The reason it's so challenging is because social profit leaders often try to fill vacancies instead of finding leaders who have skills sets and perspectives that are in alignment with the organization's strategies and goals.

When recruiting board members, leaders must look into the future of where they see their organization – not just the current day need. And, perspective board members should have the unique blend of expertise, skill set and connections that allow the organization to diversify.

So where do you start? Let's review a board recruitment strategy that many training organizations subscribe to.

Identify: Identifying board members is the first step in ramping up your social profit board. Many founders go directly to friends and family and that's a great place to start. However, it doesn't necessarily

Thyonne Gordon, Ph.D

mean start with recruiting them directly. What is more powerful is identifying people who can lead you to the people that you need. And speaking of need – have you identified what skills and the type of people that you need on your board? Yes, identification extends further than the "whom" but also associates the "what."

Think of a general type of business and the requirements of running it. Who manages the finances? Who opens the doors? Who's in charge of making sure you are legally compliant? Well, as important as those questions are to running any business they are even more important in recruiting your board. Your board members can come from all walks of life but should have two things in common – an interest in your organization and a specific reason for being identified.

Find out what your organization could use advice or support in and list that on your wish list for board members. This does not mean you will recruit an accountant to do your accounting. No, board members rarely want to give away the services that they do on a regular basis. However, they are not opposed to reviewing the work that they specialize in as part of their board role. Attorneys may offer the services of their firm on a pro-bono basis but only if it's their area of expertise and if they can get volunteers to support the efforts.

Identify your organizational needs and that will determine the type of people you need on your board. Once you've done that utilize your friends and family to help you find the people that will best suit your program. Think of identifying as if you've asked your friends and family to find you the perfect date.

Cultivate: Once you've identified the type of person you need and asked friends and family to help, begin cultivating the people that you're after. Ask them to come and see how your program works. Invite them to view your website and all materials that express your organizations mission and goals.

This is also a time for the potential board member to get to know you. Share how you became involved with your cause and what your goals are for the organization and individually. If you have children or pets, that's all a part of whom you are too. And as much sharing as you do about your organization and yourself, be sure to make lots of room to gather and learn information about this person too.

Find out what your potential board member likes and dislikes. What are their goals – career wise and personally? How do they feel they contribute or give back and what are the things that they are interested in furthering? Knowing your potential board member is an essential part of cultivation.

Once you've learned about this prospect you can then know whether they are a true prospect or not. If your organization services children and your persons' passion is around women in crisis – you may not have a match. Perhaps they will make just as good a donor than a board member. Cultivating your board member means you are figuring out how they might fit in with your organization. Remember that perfect date that your friends and family introduced you to? Well, now think about cultivating as the dating phase.

Recruit: Let's say you've identified a candidate and cultivated them enough to know that they are very keen on your cause and goals – then it's time to hit the ground with recruitment. Recruitment is not as simple as asking a person to join your board. No, recruitment is a process – just like identifying and cultivating.

Using the dating analogy, recruitment is like courtship. I know that's an "old" word but it basically means you've been

Thyonne Gordon, Ph.D

introduced to someone, you've gone out with them a couple of times and now you both have decided to see if you're interested in a long term committed relationship. That's recruitment for board members too – finding out if you want to be in a long-term committed relationship involving your organization.

To recruit your potential board member they now will not only see the programs in action but they may actually participate. Hopefully, they've already made a donation to the program but if not, this is a perfect time to discuss donations and giving. Recruitment is where the potential board member gets to "kick the tires" and it's also where you get to ask some questions and review a little deeper yourself.

Have a set period of time for recruitment of board members. Make sure they know there's a process where they can be voted to participate on the board. If you can just add people to the board at whim –

29

how special is the opportunity to sit on your board? Make sure other board members have a chance to meet with the potential board member too. After all, the board is going to be working together so they may as well like each other.

Once you've gone through some Q&A, participation and good deep conversations, give your potential candidate the time frame in which you do board elections and let them know you will add them to your slate of potential candidates. In this process be sure to give your board member a job description outlining committees and the roles that board members play.

Orient: Sealing the deal on a board member is great but it's just the start of retaining them. Make sure your new board member gets all the training they need to do the job the way you want it done. Remember understanding breeds success and making sure your board member is oriented to how you work is key.

Your existing board members should welcome new board members and if possible, take them under their wing for a mentorship. This is a good way for the new board member to begin feeling comfortable in their role. Just imagine this as your honeymoon period after sealing the deal in recruitment. Everything is new but with the right communication, you can get through anything.

Involve: New board members should get their feet wet immediately. With a lead board member encouraging them, jumping in and getting on a committee is the best way to help them acclimate. Make sure your new board member feels heard and appreciated. Ask them to participate right out the gate.

When new board members start off participating, it's easier for them to stay involved and feel needed with the organization for years to come.

Educate: Throughout the entire board process board members should be educated on new regulations in the sector as well as anything that can enhance their board experience. Subscribe to publications and media that pertain to social profit boards specifically.

Ask your board what they'd like more information on. Always have program information to share and educate your board with. As you continue to provide these learning tools to your board, you are not only sharing valuable information for their own knowledge, you are growing your organization into a powerful knowledge base.

Evaluate: Evaluating the board helps keep board members clear on their expectations. The best evaluations are self-evaluations. Allow board members to take self-evaluations on a regular basis. They should ask themselves if they are giving their all to the organization; if they have participated fully in the meeting and if they are still interested in supporting the organization as when they started. These can be difficult questions for an Executive Director to take in. However, once you know if your board members are really on board, then you can really get your organization flowing.

Rotate: Finding out where people stand through the evaluation also offers the opportunity to move things around. Rotate your board members according to your Bylaws and according to their self-evaluations. Having fresh, new people added into your board gives new perspective and a whole new network of people to learn about your organization. Don't be afraid of term limits. If there are board members who want to stay on board, make provisions for that with a break and return.

Mostly, allow those who have given great board service a chance to exit gracefully and not feel confined to being on the board forever.

Celebrate: Though this concept is written last, it's actually a part of every step. Every step of the way calls for celebration. Running a social profit is a reason to celebrate. Identifying people to participate – celebrate. Cultivating by sharing information on the organization – definitely celebrate. And then every step of the way CELEBRATE! Your board should know that you appreciate them and part of that is bringing up everything they do and celebrating it.

Find ways that you can celebrate your organization and your board – individually and collectively.

And then, start over again – and celebrate.

You're probably thinking right now that this whole process will take too long and you want to just grab a good board member. If they're professional and willing to sign up – why go through all of this right? WRONG! It is so important to go through each of these steps – even if you don't spend a substantial amount of time in each. Taking professional board members through these steps let's them know that you're a serious organization about serious business.

Having a winning plan let's people know they're part of a winning team. Make your board recruitment a winning package by exercising the steps above and assuring you have committed board members.

Chapter Three:
How Does the Board Make
It Happen

Bathroom: Each functioning bathroom tool has specific directions on how it works.

Business: Board members need specific direction on how they work.

Once you have established your board protocol and procedures of duty; recruited, cultivated and actually brought on active board members; and celebrated — it's time to validate and confirm board members are actively engaged.

Engagement is accomplished when everyone knows what work needs to be done.

Just like in the bathroom, the tools don't work without being connected to the proper vessel and then being utilized appropriately. There's a reason the shower-heads are connected to the shower arm, which allows water to flow through. With the connections properly in place, water can come down and do what it's supposed to do – give you a clean body. Now if that showerhead was placed on the sink, there wouldn't be a proper channel for the water to come through for you to have a refreshing shower!

It's the same with your board members. If they are not directed properly, the work won't get done. Or at least it won't get done as you might wish for it to get done.

The best way to keep your board on track is through the use of job descriptions. It may seem elementary or it may even seem like an over statement but job descriptions work. When you have a good job description, you know exactly what your job entails and how to reach benchmarks for success.

Why not set your board up for success with a clear and descriptive job outline. Board job descriptions often include:

- Establishing mission and purpose of new organizations or repurposing existing missions.
- Selecting the Executive Director when the position becomes available. Many times the Founder is the Executive Director, but should the position become vacant, there should be a clear path for the board to take charge of the recruitment process.
- Supporting and evaluating the Executive Director is a critical part of the board's responsibilities. An Executive Director should have a main person to report to and benchmarks for success should be established.
- Setting policies, ensuring effective planning for the organization

- Monitoring and strengthening programs and services
- Ensuring adequate financial resources through a give and get commitment to the organization
- Providing proper financial oversight by reading and thoroughly reviewing board accounting reports
- Recruiting and building a competent board; always regenerating and refueling
- Ensuring legal and ethical integrity
- Enhancing the organizations public face & standing

Having a job description makes the work of the board clear for each member. The board can then commit to the job description just like a new employee commits to a standard of conduct with their description.

Once having this clarity it's time to figure out how to get the work done that's on the job description. Because boards usually consist of several people, it's often most efficient to create committees who support the organizational work and bring results to the board at large.

A committee must have at least one person on it (though more than one makes the committee more interesting). Common committees of boards include:

- Board nominating
- Finance
- Audit
- Program Evaluation
- Fundraising
- Marketing & Public Relations
- Development strategies

There are also opportunities for ad-hoc committees that are established when needed but not necessarily active all year long. The audit committee may be an ad-hoc committee since the financial audit usually comes once a year. Other ad-hoc type committees include Building fund committee and Bylaws/Article Review.

The job of the committee is to do the legwork for the entire board to jump start activities. When a few people are in charge of presenting a plan from a committee, it means that committee has vetted the information and is bringing the best options for the board to vote on. Committees can really help boards have more effective meetings.

Meetings & Agendas

Board members must determine the timeframe in which they will meet throughout the year. Some boards meet monthly while others find quarterly to suffice with committee meetings in between. Whatever the schedule, map the time out early in the year so that there are fewer conflicts.

Remember the important work of the committee provides a wonderful way to create your agenda and move your meetings along in a productive manner.

When committees provide their reports in advance they can be added to the agenda and should there be information that is just for sharing, it can be considered as part of the a Consent Agenda.

A Consent Agenda is a practice that packages board minutes, routine committee reports, and other non-controversial and non-discussion type items, as one agenda item to be voted on at the start of the meeting. Consent agenda's save meeting time by allowing the board to approve these items together in one motion.

The consent agenda is only a viable means of reporting if all board members agree to use it and if they all vote when time to pass the consent agenda items. If even one director wants to remove an item – then it must come off the consent agenda and be reviewed in the board meeting.

Consent agenda's often include:
- Board and committee meeting minutes
- Staff reports
- Committee reports
- Final approval of document that Directors have been working on for extended time period
- Routine documents and/or contracts

Use of the consent agenda is easily adapted with the board approving a motion to adopt the consent agenda format for board meetings. As a board you can then create and approve a policy of what might be included in the consent agenda.

Most important about the consent agenda is to get documents to board members well in advance of the meeting so that they can review them and vote accordingly on the consent agenda. This also means the onus is on the board member to really review documents prior to the meeting because they will not be discussed if they are on the consent agenda.

It's a great time saver but be careful to assure board members are aware of their obligation to read documents before the meeting.

Board Leadership

Board leadership begins with the acceptance of a seat on the board of a social profit organization. Once you have decided to support an organization in this capacity understand that it's more than just a name – there are duties to be fulfilled and the way you fulfill them has a lot to do with how the board is structured and how each member steps into leadership.

Some common ways of taking leadership is to assume an officer position on the board. The most common officers – and the ones needed on every board are:

President or Chairman/Chairwoman of the board. In this capacity the member leads the board in their activities. In conjunction with the Executive Director of the organization, this person sets the board agenda (including the consent agenda); they corroborate with leads of board committees; review and become very familiar with financials; keep strong relationships with other board members; run the meetings; and (normally) supervise and evaluate the Executive Director on behalf of the board. Though all of these duties are important and self-explanatory, the supervision and evaluation of the Executive Director by one person, demands further investigation for the health of the organization.

The importance of one person (the Chair or a Personnel Committee lead) being the direct supervisor for the Executive Director, falls in line with parts being connected properly in a bathroom. Yes, I'm back to the bathroom analogies!

Imagine your toilet taking direction from the sink, bathtub and shower handles in your bathroom in addition to the commode flushing mechanisms. What a mess this could create! The toilet would be flushing repeatedly with the turn of any bathroom fixture handle. Eventually, it would break down from overload, a broken handle or leak. And the owner would break down too when they saw the excessive water bill!

A breakdown of the Executive Director is just the start of problems when leaders are not given proper direction in the social profit world. Without one person to report to directly, Executive Directors could be responding to an entire board of 10 to 20 people – all at one time. That means on even a 5 person board the social profit leader would potentially have 5 bosses! With so many potential bosses, there is the potential that the Executive Director would be expected to report timely, accurately and efficiently all the time to varied requests. This leaves no time for the Executive to manage his/her team and thus is not fair to the organization, the board members needing support and especially not the person at the helm of such important work. Figure out whom your Executive will report to and schedule timely evaluations with set benchmarks for the Executive. Though the Executive is reporting to one person, they are duty bound to the entire board. That is why the Chairperson is generally the person handling this task since they work together to facilitate board activities. A good board Chair can help their Executive find balance in how they work with the board by tasking board members to complete work outside the use of organizational manpower and staying in constant communication with the Executive.

Vice-Chair or Vice President: This board member supports the efforts of the Chairperson/President assisting in setting agenda's; working with committee leads or any of the other functions that the Chair/President does. The Vice-Chair can also be assigned specific duties (i.e. committee supervision or E.D. supervision) as a standing part of the position, as a standing committee or as an ad-hoc. The Vice-Chair serves as a sounding board for the Chair/President in moving forward with the work of the board.

Treasurer: This position is one of the most confusing to many social profits. Many believe it requires accounting to be done. This is not true. Organizations must have their own Accountants or Bookkeepers. This position is more of a reviewer of the financials. The treasurer should understand how to read financials and what they mean so that they can help relay the information to the board. As treasurer, one would work closely with the Accountant of the organization to gather the proper financials that the entire board should review regularly. This consistency is different for each organization. Some organizations have quarterly review while others do monthly. The treasurer can help determine the reviewing of the reports. It is also important that the treasurer be fully aware of the financial health of the organization and assist in relaying that information to the board for review.

The officer positions above comprise the governing officers or what is often called an executive committee. Executive committees can also include other board members. All other board members participate as general or regular members who support the organization through programming, revenue building and maintaining, marketing and recruitment. As a board member, duties vary but consistently members should be prepared to:

- Attend regularly scheduled meetings
- Participate in meetings
- Review financials and offer

recommendations
- Generate revenue for organization
- Participate in fundraising events or activities
- Participate on one or more committees

Serving on a board of directors is an honor and a job. Be accepting to the fact that you are a change maker for the organization you serve and serve it well.

Summary

If you find yourself in the position of Board Chair or Executive Director, congratulations – you're the gas station or house that the bathroom resides in. Be flexible and tap into whatever motivates you to be of service.

Start strong, identify the organizational values and mission, define your board roles and get to work. Be ready to bring your ideas, opinions and strategies to the table. You are a champion for the organization! Everyone looks to your steady, strong presence. Don't disappoint them by being "out of order" or "closed for cleaning." Know what you are supposed to do and get it done.

As the steady holding tank of the organization, be visionary but stay on point with your mission. Have job descriptions for your board members. Take care with the duty of care, duty of loyalty and the duty of obedience. Most importantly, enjoy your board service by being fully active with the organization and the other volunteer board members that serve with you.

Most important, whether a board member, volunteer or working on an ad-hoc committee -- enjoy your board experience. It is one of the most gratifying and rewarding experiences of a lifetime.

www.ingramcontent.com/pod-product-compliance
Lightning Source LLC
Chambersburg PA
CBHW071639040426
42452CB00009B/1696